THE FUTURE

THE FUTURE

Poems by

NEIL HILBORN

◇◇◇

Published by Button Poetry / Exploding Pinecone Press

Minneapolis, MN 55403 | http://www.buttonpoetry.com

◇◇◇

Cover Design: Nikki Clark

ISBN 978-1-943735-31-0

CONTENTS

IV

When someone stops before they begin performing a poem to explain—it's not done yet, I'm not sure how I feel, I might cut this intro—I always say "No disclaimers." The poem needs to speak for itself, and whatever you don't like, you can change. Whatever you change, that will speak for itself too. The poem has to have a life of its own without you telling me what that life is.

Having said all that, let me say this: I wrote so much of this book when I was on the road. For the past four years I have been touring and performing professionally, so many of the poems in this book were written in places like Macomb, Illinois and Farmville, Virginia. Yes, no kidding, in Virginia there is a place called Farmville, and it was a super chill town with a cool little college that hosted one of my top ten favorite shows I've done. I always joke that I'm a professional driver who sometimes gets to perform poems, so a lot of what you see here I wrote while taking a break from driving from one place I'd never heard of to another. I wrote this book in rest stops off 77 in the Alleghenies, and I wrote this book in Iowa when I was too tired from fighting the wind, the wheel and the car determined to dive through the fence and into the fields, the fields, the fields. I wrote this book when I could and because I had to.

Every book has to go through an editing process. Kerouac would have liked you to believe that *On the Road* was spontaneous and unchanged, but come on now. Before I collected all these poems together and sent them to someone with the note "Please make this not terrible," they were all edited by every audience I stepped in front of. In 2016 I performed at over 100 shows, and every poem in here is one that went in front of at least a few of those crowds. An audience is an incredible editor if you're paying attention. Just the energy you get back from them will let you know which lines are working, which aren't, where your poem is too fast or slow, and which poems are, despite your immense love for them, not very good. This book has had countless editors, and if you came to a show, I want to thank you for helping these poems be not only what they are, but what they always had the potential to be.

So I guess this really isn't a disclaimer—I love this book, and I think you will too—this is more of an explanation. Most of this book was written all over America, and there is still so much more America that I will never get to see. It's hard to build a life back home when you spend so much of your time staring at the horizon. So to anyone in any small town who poured me a coffee or sold me a new handkerchief, anyone who came to a show and allowed me to both struggle and succeed, anyone going the other way on a back road who waved, raising their fingers slightly off the wheel, thank you, and this one is for you.

I

The relief, always, of you in the seat beside me, you'll never know.

—GRETCHEN MARQUETTE

Nothing ever absolutely has to happen.

—MATT RASMUSSEN

There was so much to think about if you just gave yourself the time, even in places most people couldn't find on a map.

—JOHN DARNIELLE

HOW DO YOU SLEEP WITH AN IV IN?

It's just for dehydration, the nurse
says. She hangs up this alien bladder
full of fluid so clear that it couldn't
possibly be from anywhere but space.

A little of your blood slides up
the tube before it retreats under
the rushing tide of whatever is
in that loud bag. I know you probably

won't die. You won't, definitely,
but I'm great at catastrophizing
so why stop here? I'm sure the doctor
is going to turn to me and say

that you have something incurable.
The nurse is great at not wanting anyone
to panic, but when she walks back
into the room and sees your first bag

almost gone, her eyes go
wide for one moment, as though
you had just fallen limp
onto the tracks. The doctor asks me

three times before we leave
if I understand just how much
ibuprofen, that he means it
when he says as much liquid

as you can stomach. He says
it's hard to care for someone
as sick as you are and I'm a great
boyfriend, and I say nothing

about the ring I bought you
or the box it lives in again,
nothing about how you were
supposed to move out tomorrow

and how we're supposed to take
things slow, and we will, we'll talk
slow, eat slow, reveal everything
we've kept hidden, just like that, slow,

and there I am at four AM, drifting
into what was our bedroom like a thief
holding water and pills, and there I am
also shuffling back to the couch and turning

off the lights, he doesn't have
to know that tomorrow
you'll cancel the movers as well
as the wedding venue, all

the invitations unmailed, no dress
yet, thank god, here's her prescription,
remember her fluids, she'll be fine
in a week, have a nice day.

BIG GOLD JUKEBOX

I'm seventeen maybe and the Jeep
used to be gold. What's the color
gold becomes? Anyway this car
was magic or maybe my dad
was a wizard because every song
I asked him for was up next
on the radio. I wanted Journey
and there they were, twelve guitars
and melodrama. That Jeep made it
to a couple punk shows before it went
to Jeep heaven, a particularly nice
junkyard, and I'm trying to show
Brent and Nathan and Paul and Kayleigh
the trick, check it, just want something
hard enough and you'll hear it. In about two
minutes you can have some Clash or Cars,
bands it's reasonable to expect, okay
who wanted Aerosmith, you're walking
home. Maybe magic is real but it stops
when you turn sixteen. Maybe travel
at high speed is all the mystery
adults get. Maybe I traded spells
for a Bluetooth connection, now any song
is just there whenever. There's no time
between wanting and having. The air is
a poor conductor now and the ideas
used to fall out of it. The Jeep
is a time machine and in it is your father.
You're going to soccer or swimming or home
and everything you need will be here
soon. You have to wait, but not for very long.

REVENGE SEX

I'm working on erasing you,
I just don't have the proper tools.
—FRIGHTENED RABBIT

You have to fuck
like there is nothing left
to lose. There, of course, is,
but it's pretty hard to make
someone orgasm when you're trying
to remember what you paid
for the couch.

HEAR ROCKS SING ON GREAT STALACTITE ORGAN

Virginia, probably. North Carolina
maybe. Pack the car before dawn, bring
what you think you'll need: gun oil,
compass, map of what could be under
the world, written in dreams and made
flesh. Paper can be flesh here, now,
at the end of this fifth age. Bring the spikes
in case it snows under the earth. Bring
the chains and whatever other metal
you can find. Turn yourself in. Get lost
on the way home. Get out the mallet
and grip tape. Sewing needle, green
thread, syringe, black iron, heated
in fire. Diesel fuel, dusk at four pm.
Wet floor, who knows how. The window
is broken and all the leaves are coming
home. Here at the end of the dirt road,
at the mouth of the Shenandoah Valley,
head into the cave where the rocks are
singing. This is what the whole drive
was for. All the gasoline fumes
and truck stop food was so, right here,
the rocks could make this noise.

THE BALLAD OF FUCKKNUCKLE JONES

Mark is the kind of guy who,
given the opportunity, would never
lock his car. If you've ever driven
two blocks farther than you meant to
and parked cause you're good there, that's
Mark. Mark has a spare room

and I'm sleeping in it until I know
exactly how apart everything is
going to fall. Mark says I can stay
as long as I need and I believe
him, but also I am cleaning each
plate immediately after I use it.

If you ever need someone to drive you
to a firing squad, ask Mark. He's the kind
of guy who, when he says you'll be
fine, is probably right. The end isn't
coming soon, just what's next, and Mark
is gonna be there, turning the record over, raising
a middle finger, keeping the car running.

VOCABULARY

I hear that in Hungarian they don't
say "Go to hell" but rather "I hope

I'm there when your children decide
they don't need you anymore." In Scotland

the popular greeting is "Have you eaten
the heart of the mountain?" In America we should

say "You must leave town at midnight" for both
Yes and No, but we don't have the balls, which should

only be an adjective for cheese and lightning,
I'm sorry. If there's a word for the slight glow

of a lightbulb after you've turned it off, I don't
want to know it. There should be a way to say "Fuck you"

that's actually sexy. I hear the ancient Egyptians
would spread crocodile dung on sandstone tablets,

and when they scraped it off, there were the words.
The word for tomorrow was a stork, flying away.

What's the word for a place that you loved,
a window seat, a garden, a house of stone,

a wall in a field you were carried to on the wind,
that, when you look for it again, is gone.

AND MISSED

And then it was the day
I tried to sleep all day
and missed. And then
the day, probably the same
day, that I couldn't take
the bunny out of her cage
even though she was right
there, even though she was giving
me the look that says she wants to
cuddle, because I know
that when I leave
she is not going
with me, and I can't
start loving her more now.

Hey man, don't do this to me again. I thought we were cool.

—THE ONE PAIR OF UNDERWEAR NEIL
BROUGHT ON TOUR

Please play something else. I'm fucking exhausted.

—THE SENSES FAIL CD THAT'S BEEN ON
REPEAT SINCE DENVER

Help! Can anyone hear me?! I'm stuck! It's pretty bad.

—NEIL'S WEDGIE THAT'S BEEN GETTING
WORSE SINCE CLEVELAND

TWO DAYS IN WILLIAMSPORT, PA

You ever stay because it's easier
than going? You ever decide
by not deciding? I meant to go
East into the ocean but that was before
I found the Moon and Raven. There was
a scotch and a steak, the scotch
was like drinking a campfire
next to a tire fire, and then it was
two days later and I had to leave
for Albany. Well no, things happened,
but they weren't, well, there are only
so many ways to talk about eating cheese
and crackers while watching History
Channel "documentaries" about how
Hitler is still alive, only so many
trudges through the melting
snow, because it's always March
in Williamsport, so many drives
past the modest Victorian
homes shivering together
on their hill, with the windows
just slightly down, the music up
halfway. No singing because it feels
disrespectful to care about anything
in all this grey, all this slush
everywhere, somewhere
you could live but won't.

REVENGE SEXY

Now that I'm done crying
into the pillow that smells
like you, I've decided to care
about how I look again. I'm not
saying that contentment makes me
gain weight, but I do look vaguely
like I'm me twice. So I'm gonna
get so hot that everyone's Tinder
will just show my face. If you swipe
left long enough the picture will
slowly start crying. I'm gonna
look so good that the beach
will be renamed the me.
I'm gonna get arm veins
and a whole bunch of grey
pubes. I wanna look
distinguished yet violent. I wanna
climb a tree and then chop
it down. I'm gonna make statues
come to life, slap each other,
then smush face. Turns out
spontaneous human combustion
is real. Someone get a camera.
I'm gonna lift weights and burst
into flames.

I DON'T NEED TO HAVE A BETTER DAY, I NEED TO FEEL BETTER ABOUT THIS ONE

There is some truth to what Hieu once said
about how a lot of the time I don't want to

die, I'm just embarrassed and that makes me
long for death. Not death, just not being

here. I would rather die than confront
my mistakes, and I spent

long enough fixing nothing so I could
feel nothing that now it's just mistakes

all the way down. So yes, when tasked with admitting
something is wrong I do genuinely consider

how much it is going to disrupt the already precarious
life I built for myself. Just a slight push

from embarrassment might be enough to tip
over this wheezing, expensive machine, if my things

are going to be scattered all over the street, why not
leave before I see them thrown? I know, I do,

that I feel this way now and will not
feel this way soon. I know that

the aphorisms, even if I hate them,
are right. This too shall pass. Blah blah

darkest blah blah dawn. And I know
it's rude to leave your messes for someone

else, but consider also that I am a mess
and I make people deal with me pretty

constantly. Consider that most every day
is me crying alone in a car or bedroom over

nothing, goddamn nothing, and consider
that this is supposed to get better as I get older

and it's getting worse, no one warned me
I would just get more anxious, consider the future,

and how I've seen it, and maybe it's not
worth seeing again.

ALTERNATE UNIVERSE IN WHICH MY FATHER DID NOT LEAVE BUT DIED

We are coming back from the funeral
and I am thirteen, maybe. I've never
seen his hair not in a ponytail. I know
I was supposed to say something
to him in the casket, but there isn't
a word that means goodbye and I'll miss
you and please come back to me somehow
and let me know when you get there?
My mother scrapes leftovers
into our largest tupperware. My mother
vacuums the carpet four times. She sits
facing the front door as though that would
ever be the one he'd walk through. Back
from a business trip. Back for good
this time, he says. The research
is done, the investors are happy, we can
go back to Mexico any time we want
now that it's over, he says, now that
it's all over and done. I'd almost rather
he just left us. Maybe in another life
he just found someone new and I can
see him sometimes for basketball games
or dinner on Saturdays. Maybe in that life
I love what I have and what I have isn't gone.

KARINA

Karina is the kind of girl who has
no idea where you live, but can tell you
where to find every bar that's opened

in the last two months. Which is not
to say that she drinks a lot, but that she likes
to be the kind of cool person who can tell

you where to go be cool. Karina and I kissed
once, but that was at least four haircuts ago
and I can barely even remember where I lived

back then. Once Karina drove with us
to New Jersey and I honestly didn't know
it could take an hour and a half

to do your makeup just to get across
Pennsylvania. Karina just wants to get married, she
always has, and who am I to say that

happiness has to be something you find
on your own, or a door after hallways
made of doors, and in a different life I wouldn't

have been like I am or dumped her
after two months, in that life we bought
a house in Iowa, Wisconsin, somewhere

close to her parents, they're coming over
for dinner. I'm making pork chops with
applesauce. I got the apples right from

the garden; the guest room is always clean.

PLACES TO NEVER RETURN

College, because I'm not creepy
and reunions are terrible; the hat shop
that I didn't exactly get fired from
but like; your mom's house haha;
Kentuckiana; really any basement
ever, and there have been a lot
of basements (venues, apartments,
illegal bars, tunnels, bedrooms,
storage); the house I grew up in,
I think that's finished now; the backyard
where the trees began speaking; the sheets
in which the bad thing happened;
where I was in love, probably, at least
that's what I said.

ALTERNATE UNIVERSE IN WHICH MY BARBER, GIB, WHO ONCE GAVE ME A MUSCLE CAR CALENDAR, IS MY GRANDFATHER

You know, Grampa always makes
fun of the people who sit in those
uncomfortable-ass bench chairs. He says
they've been there since the eighties
and probably haven't been cleaned
since the seventies. Everyone who is
anyone sits in the lawn chairs. You know,
like the mayor. Grampa says he gets
shaves here all the time. You're
right, that fridge is full of Cokes,
but there's a row of Bud Lights
in the back. You know, for special
occasions like when your Army buddies
aren't dead. I'm going in today
so Grampa can touch me up
with the straight razor. Nah, he never
nicked anybody with that razor
who didn't deserve it. Nazis, mostly.
Yeah, lots of skinheads in St Paul,
to hear Grampa tell it. Says all
the rich kids wanna be poor kids
and all the poor kids wanna be
dead. Anyway, wanna come with?
There's usually a spot open
out back. I'm sure Grampa would
love to see you, but you don't
even have to come in. You could
just nap right there in the car.

RUST BELT

There's something about a boarded-up
window that says "come here." Plywood,
nails, spray paint, no lights, above all quiet.
Bricks, apples, and rust aren't red. Red is a place
called Indianapolis. Places should begin
and have weight. Places should be full
of light and kitchens and clean sheets,
but Indianapolis wouldn't know a dinner
table. Somewhere in Indy is a brick street
that's never needed repair. The grocery stores
are just knee-high empty shelves. You have
to, as always, ask for what you want. It's never
rained here, only snowed, but snow can melt,
you know. You can always melt, so either
drive on by or start to fade away.

THE DOOR

after Hieu Minh Nguyen and Sara Brickman

The hard part, probably, is admitting
that I really can't handle it
anymore. I can't just hire someone
to take care of the two-year-old
unpaid parking tickets. I threw money
at my loneliness and all I got
were friends who think of drunk driving
as a sport. I stared at my phone
for so long that I grew
a glass face. First you say you feel
nothing, then your eyes start to
agree with you, then one day
someone you love, probably,
cries in front of you and your only
thought is "When is dinner." There is
only one way left to talk about
being sad that won't make me
more sad: I'm so sad I jumped off
a bridge and missed. I'm so sad
that one time I called my therapist
"Mom." I've made enough jokes
about killing myself that I'm starting
to think they're funny. Every time I say
"goodbye" I find myself adding "forever"
because who knows when it will be
true. The text message is a lightbulb
on a bad wire. I start typing
and the ellipses flicker. If I say,
delete, if I, delete, the filament
pops and the whole light sleeps. Tomorrow
is a lease I have to sign every
morning. Get me a carrier pigeon. Fire

up the old telegraph. Open the window
and let me shout for help: something is
burning, bring water bring water I'm so sad
I fell in love with hands and a row
of teeth. I'm so sad I line up the knives
and stare until one of them speaks.
Where's the bad part, how do I carve
it out, by now is it all rot?

LAKE

There's a fire somewhere down
river. Just a thin arm of grey reaching
up from the river flats. The Lake Street Bridge
always gives me vertigo. The water probably
isn't that far away, you can sort of see the expressions

of the people on boats below you, if you dropped
a rock onto the sand it wouldn't make
too deep a hole, I guess. I've got to go home

now but I'm sitting outside my old home. When
does home emerge from just the place where I put
all my stuff? The new house is where I do
all my living, so I guess the old house is where
I'm dead. I've been saying all that so I didn't have to

say this: it's too easy to jump off a bridge
or take some pills. No, actually, you've got to
walk to the bridge so no one tows your

mom's car. You've got to buy or steal
the pills. Mostly it's too easy to go without
saying goodbye. Yes, there is a place
where someone loves you both before
and after they learn what you are.

That place is called the world, and if
you want to live it's really the only
option. You could choose not to, but then

where would you get really great
sandwiches or listen to Springsteen
with the windows down? When you
want to cry you'll have to just not. Yes
people will miss you, but if you've wanted

to kill yourself for a while you've heard that too
much and it no longer means anything. "Goodbye"
isn't a strong enough word, but "fuck off

forever" isn't always what I mean.
Listen, if I joke about wanting to kill myself
that means I don't want to do it. Start
worrying when I only talk about brunch
and dog breeds. Start worrying whenever

you want, really, I'm not your boss. I don't
know why I asked my phone how to get
home from here, but I guess it's nice
when someone else agrees with me. The GPS
says it will take three minutes. Home is where

I most comfortably have panic attacks. When I get
home I get to stay there. I get to sleep, then
I get to, if I want to, do this all again.

I have no idea when he wrote this. He literally spent all day yesterday googling "Neil Hilborn unicorn fan fiction."

—NEIL'S PHONE

He's writing something! He's finally doing it! Wait, wait...nope he's just signing his name again.

—NEIL'S NOTEBOOK

Wheeeee I'm a bike! I'm a bike! Wheee!

—NEIL'S BIKE

NEXT EXIT

It was come home, go to sleep, get up, go to work, don't look at each other.
—PATTON OSWALT

A Red Bull can with a Band-Aid
in it. A speed limit sign and a dented
bumper. The guard rails and new patches
on asphalt, the orange stripes next to
the white. The shoulder and my broken
shoulder, both crunch when they move.
The world takes forever to get
across. The world is a place full
of uncomfortable beds. Before all this
I had an idea, and ideas are made mostly
for being wrong, but I had an idea that
every town would have something
about it. The thing about the world
is that most of it is actually terrible,
and believing that every small town
is imbued with quiet dignity
is a disservice to both people
and dignity. So let places be bad
if they're bad. If there weren't
awful places to be from
there'd be nowhere to grow up
and run away from. So if you're bored
be bored. Get to the dock. Lean out
over the rail. Stay until you can't
stay no more. Turn the key and then
the engine. Let the world pass
beneath your wheels and never
think of it again.

SO LONG

Back home it snowed
on Halloween, have you
ever. Have you ever heard
the sound someone makes
when they've decided
to cut themselves off, either
at the bar or at the knees?
They're the same sound, and that's
a word probably, in the way
words are sounds we've all agreed
mean no, this chair or see you
soon maybe or I don't want
to be here I can't stay. How do I
describe sound proofing that doesn't
work. A flight delayed by the passengers.
Uninsulated windows, the corner
room and the broken radiator, sleeping
better when your feet are cold. How do
we know instinctively when it's time
to leave a party? There isn't a song
that plays, just the host in the kitchen
drying glasses. I'm kidding I've never
been to a party where I drank
out of a glass, never been sober
enough to care that someone wanted
me to go, but I've never walked
into any room and wanted to stay.

ODE TO ME, FROM MY DENIM VEST

You dumb sweaty idiot. My collar
is fraying and there's a condom
in my inside pocket. Have

you ever like ever heard of
a washing machine? I'd like
to be in one. Put me in
one for a year, bro. You can't

just use me as your security
blanket and then decide
it's ok to live in filth. Filth

is not secure you dumb dummy.
I could be covered in patches
and pyramid studs. I could be
a blanket for a pitbull. If I am

gonna be dirty all the time
I should at least be badass,
I should be inspiring, even if
only of fear and nausea

but no, I've gotta go with you
to Kansas City or central Maine,
I've gotta wait

for you in your bag when you get
too warm. I'll wait until the stitches
burst and it all falls off, because

I love you, stupid. I can't not.
I've been falling apart since I was
born but now I have you. Come here,
let me hold you.

AGAINST HUGS

I make so many decisions
because other people expect
me to. I cut my hair
and go to expensive bars
with terrible music, but today
what I would like to focus on is
hugs. I've been in so many
subcultures where if you didn't
hug someone you hated them,
and that made sense
when I was a punk kid
or a fencer because those
are already violent sports
and when you've had
someone's blood on you,
what's a little chest touching?
But now I'm a poet,
all my friends are poets,
and unless they've been lying to me
a lot of them are introverts, and unless
everyone has been lying to me
I'm pretty sure introverts aren't
all about hugs. So basically
when my visibly uncomfortable friends
and I, visibly uncomfortable, hug,
we are two introverts doing some
extrovert shit because some
extroverts might possibly be around,
and I'll admit that it's useful
to blend in so no one can see
you crying or plotting against them,
it's more useful to make people
feel loved, your happiness is
probably worth my slight discomfort,
fine, hey buddy, come here.

I'M BACK, NOT FOR GOOD

You ever been punched in the neck
and liked it? That's what it's like
to walk out of baggage claim in Houston
in August. It's hard to be sad
at my grandma's funeral when I'm
trying to breathe soup. It's also
hard to be sad because my grandmother
was a horrible woman who abused
my mom and all my aunts
and uncles, but it's easier to blame
the weather. How telling is it
that at the wake the only one crying
is my aunt by marriage. She's looking
at me like I'm a very mean
monster every time I laugh,
which is often, because my cousin
who also isn't sad is hilarious in that way
only librarians can be. You can't
be all about books without basically
becoming one. My grandma
was dying for the last eighth
of her life, so everyone in this room
wearing black and holding these plastic
cups, everyone expected to be here
much sooner than this. I thought
it couldn't be long when I visited
her at the nursing home where she was
already so done that she could only
form one syllable, said it over
and over, where my mom fed her
chocolate, some of it melted
and dribbled out of the side of her
mouth that she couldn't move, I
pretended not to notice until my

mom saw because I didn't feel
capable of wiping it away, I thought
then it won't be long, and that
was years ago. So tonight I'll get
drunk on and then sleep on
my brother's couch. In the morning
I'll head to the airport, having fixed
or resolved nothing, because I'm
always back, but not for good.

ODE TO THE GASLIGHT ANTHEM, ENDING IN THE END OF CHILDHOOD

after Hanif Abdurraqib

There's no summer better than the summer before you turn eighteen. It felt like it was terrible for a reason. All the self-hatred was finally going somewhere, like all that time I spent veering toward and then away from guard rails was so I could find new bridges somewhere north. The North is mythical and covered in ice. It's ice, dirt, then ice all the way down. There's nowhere close enough that you could get there by train, and isn't that what it means to stop running away, stranding yourself somewhere so hard that it has to work, it has to and if it doesn't there's only back south or the snow. The snow spreads its arms and yawns. The snow starts saying goodnight the moment it wakes. South is where they love you but no matter where you drive it's always into the sun and the sun doesn't bat its eyes at you the way it used to, the sun only spreads its arms and yawns but you don't shine like you used to, you used to be a glittering machine, you were brand new and so sharp and hungry for fingers and now who could tell you from dirty snow, look at you there all pale and nonstop bruises, in you somewhere is still that teenager with the rough and bloody voice, angry with the radio on, driving nowhere, and where would that loud idiot go if he knew he would one day turn into you?

FOR HENRY, WHO HAS JUST GONE

Henry was my pet rat, and he died
last night in my hands. He was three
years old, which is way longer than

an albino rat is supposed to live. To be
honest, he wasn't a very smart animal,
but he was so sweet that now I wonder

if intelligence has anything to do
with leading a good life. He had been sick
for a few months, and every twelve hours

I had to apply antiseptic and lotion
to both his back feet. By the end
they didn't really work anymore,

so he would just drag his feet behind him in a way
so cute and sad that I started calling him my little
sea lion. When he died it was, somehow,

a surprise: you would think that when your rat
is older than older than dirt and has been sick for months
you'd be sort of prepared: after I had laid out the towel

and mixed the solution, I picked him
up and noticed his breathing
was so slow. I lay down with him

on the towel, the towel where we'd spent
the last few months, where I think we
finally, really, completely, loved each other,

not like humans do: humans always want
something from you and he and I
would just rather be together than apart,

and I pulled him toward me, and he chittered in that way
that always meant he was wind coming in after a rain,
his head fell forward, and there was so much less

light in the room. The lamp was so far away,
like the light of a house to which there is no
road. I know, he was just a rat. So many

just like him, all white, red eyes,
die every day and only one or two people
in white coats are even there to see it.

He was all in white, he was always there
to see me. When I would wake from a nightmare,
so many nightmares, I would turn on the light

and there he was, holding on, a constant companion
to a prisoner, the prison being the apartment,
the world being inside his cage. Once I was crying

in bed because of who knows why, and he sat beside my
face and licked my tears away. I had a rat
once, named Henry. Named Buddy. Named Mr. Big

Mouse. Named proof that something could need me
and still love me. Named please
can I have some of your apple? Or I know

you're sad but I'm hungry. Don't go, if you go
I won't survive: a child reaches for her father;
a couple, buried in ash, dies holding each other;

a man and a woman in an office, crying slightly,
sign sheets of paper; sparrows fall out of the sky together.
Some day I'm going to have a child. She's going to have

eyes like mine and such small hands. Just like
she'll need me alive then, she needs me alive
now; I can't say goodbye before I've had a chance

to say hello. I don't stare off bridges anymore.
I don't count out little blue exit signs and even today,
with Henry buried under a tree, a tree somewhere so far away

it feels like someone else buried him using my body,
today I came home and only wanted to sleep
for twenty minutes instead of always. Something needed

me once, and I know something will need me
again. One day I'm going to have a daughter.
She's going to sleep through the night

sometimes. She is a light on a rock
at the edge of a lonely sea. You see that light
out there? That's where I'm headed. That's home.

ODE TO BRAIN INJURIES

You big dumb light. You scrambled

eggs intended over easy. You small
ocean in a small world. I was never

sure, and then I met you. Now I'm not

sure that I'm never sure. I used to be
bricks on other bricks. Now I'm a screen

going dark. I'm a meal for four

spread over the tile. You don't wake me
in the night. You don't have to

kiss me because you're always

kissing me. Here is what it's like
to sleep while you're awake.

A HISTORY OF PUNK ROCK

A guy who was mad at his parents
threw a rock at a loom and that was the first
circle pit. Someone smashed a new
oxcart into an old oxcart

and the stage dive was born. Four chords
used to mean four chords, fighting
in the wind. The straight edge
knew what it would one day

become. Woody Guthrie painted
some shit on his guitar and didn't know
what to call it but protest music. I wore
basketball shorts and kicked my friends

in their heads and I don't know
how to explain myself so now
I just say I was punk. There aren't
going to be new ways to hate

yourself, so you might as well
get hurt with your friends. I've never
been someone I could be proud of,
but in thirty years I'll be telling

some children about doing front flips
off some stage in some basement somewhere
in Minneapolis, and the new way to not
give a shit will be listening

to your elders, so they'll ask what it was
like to watch a middle-aged man
in a luchador mask sing/scream
about Michael Jackson, and I'll try

to tell them about rocks and looms
and black sails in the sunset
but I've taken so many shots
to the face that I might not be me

tomorrow, or Wednesday, there's no
good way to talk about the true
believers, even if I can't remember
I was there, I was me, I was there.

KISSES

First

It's 2004 maybe and we have
just come back from the Renaissance

Festival. Emily, which is probably
how you spell her name, is wearing

a handmaiden's dress of my mother's
that we will never see again. Light blue

skirt, almost white blouse, freshwater
pearls so small they could be snow

evenly spaced over the bodice, and
she was done with me two days later

so goodbye. It's always a long drive

home and Emmalee has fallen
asleep on my shoulder. As we pull

into her driveway I shake her
as though she is or could predict my

future. So I'm pretty sure
my mom watched my first kiss,

which was tender, anxious, and over
too soon, like most of how it's been

to live.

Best

It was one hour into my birthday and I had
finally finally finally

convinced Emily, no not
the first, another, to wander away with me

from all our friends, the other poets
with their needful and crying eyes and it started

raining and so we found a bridge
to stand under and our legs were covered

in dirt and the whole world smelled
like metal earth, just like her makeup, just like

the blood in my face she held
my hand the whole way back, well

not the whole way, we could hear our friends
with about a block to go, and that's where our

fingers fell off I mean away away and away.

BLOOD IN MY SOCK

I was making completely
normal, absolutely not
drunk decisions, and I fucked up
my toe. Now the nail
is attempting an escape.
Let me back up. It's Friday
night and I've been
convinced to go out
with people, which I never do,
especially not on a weekend.
Everyone knows that
if you hate yourself you drink
on Tuesday. So completely
normal, definitely sober me
is biking home because drunk
biking is as close as science
will come to time travel
in my life. I'm in some
neighborhood in Saint Paul
where the streets are empty
so I can better practice
my Tom Waits voice, you gotta
close your eyes to get the growl
right, which is why I don't
see the rather large pothole
that eats my front wheel. If this
pothole had been any
bigger it would have been
called a fault line. Admittedly,
I should have heard this pothole
blocks away because of the screams
of the damned emanating from it,
but I was singing about dead birds
and broken umbrellas. Thank god

it's midnight because I'm gonna lay
in the middle of this street until
I can rationalize the decisions
that brought me here. Not just the booze
but the decision to be a bike person
and the decision to move
to Minnesota and all
the decisions to continue living.
I'm gonna stay here until I become
a rock under a lot of other
rocks, a copper pot that's only
every been used for cooking, a light
that knows it won't go out. I'm staying
here until I love myself. It's only
a few blocks home, so I trudge it
with blood in my sock. I'm walking
with one foot in the ocean.

ALL AGES

Mom, why would you remember this, but you
bought me my first punk record. It was
No Control, and that's how I know when
to properly use words like fecundity

and trammel, so I guess
in case you weren't already aware,
you're probably a large part of why
I am truly insufferable. But anyway,

that laser and the headphones. That cross
crossed out. Mom if I hadn't found
punk I'd be dead but also my jaw
would work. I would have gotten to it

without you, but it might have taken
longer, and that might have meant nothing
or that might have meant nothingness.
So now we're still both here and we are

not dead, and Mom, what's more punk rock
than living despite all that
which has tried to make you not?

FUTILITY MACHINE

after Dislexia by Ivan Capote

What about a road that only ever
turns. What about your life,
the same every time. Change
the fonts and margins if you think
that will get you across
the bridge. Don't make
pronouncements and then say
you're not a liar. Nothing you know
will be true in a year or so. If you
go home it might not be home
anymore or maybe it will be
home, just not yours.

BRUCE SPRINGSTEEN WILL NEVER DIE

Some people are forces rather than
people, you know? Obviously that is
reductive, Springsteen is his own
person and leads his own private life,
but I'll never see that so I don't have to
mention it here. I don't mean that Bruce
will live on through his music or whatever
bullshit corny people say, I mean that
he is too important to not be alive. I mean
that it must have sucked for everyone
who was alive before he was born
kind of in the same way that some Christians
think that everyone who lived before
Jesus automatically went to hell, how
rude. I mean that the Reaper has Nebraska
in his top five albums and won't take The Boss
because He also likes going to arena shows
in Jersey. Born to Run is a better album
than I am a person; even if
it hurts you it knows how to build
you back up. It's going to be lonely
for Bruce when we're all gone. The screen
door slams, it's never Mary anymore,
now it's just the wind.

GET UP EARLY, GET TO THE DOCK

There's no clear way to describe how asphalt
makes the air unsure of itself in August. The cicadas

live underground for seventeen years and then one day
they all decide to turn your neighborhood into

a soundtrack titled Jet Engines of the Lower Americas.
Some time this summer that muddy lake out there

is going to get another itself dumped into itself. You've
never been canoeing until you've floated one down

your own street, so sometimes Houston is the Venice
of places where people sit in traffic all the time. You've never

seen ants until you've seen a raft of ants, biting on to
one another for security. Somewhere in the middle is a queen,

covered in bodies. It's rumored that in the tunnels
under downtown there's a leprechaun covered

in barbecue sauce who will answer your wishes but only
if they are meat-related but I digress. Once I lived

in that lake. I had fallen in the water and the boat
just kept going. I wasn't sure anyone would notice

I wasn't still there, coming up with more puns about docks
and the shoreline. There are worse ways to go than a propeller

or a long row of teeth and scales. The next hurricane, consider
staying home. It might be the end, but before that, you'll fly.

IV

Who is this man? I've never seen him in my life.

—NEIL'S SHOWER

It's like looking into a mirror.

— NEIL'S GARBAGE CAN

MOVE-IN DAY

The first time it was you, holding all your boxes outside of that first "garden level" we hated. It's sort of fun to hate something when it's yours, you know? Anyway, this time it's me, having drawn all of my possessions from that basement they lived in during my time in exile, and I don't know how we thought all our stuff could fit into this tiny apartment when we first picked it out, back before I said anything about my doubts, my doubts, god, they feel so stupid now, now that we've learned how to say to each other more than "I'm afraid." Now my only doubt is that all our clothes will get into this closet. I might have to get rid of some books. Small price for knowing I get to sleep next to you again.

AS MUCH WIND AS POSSIBLE

So because of the chemical
imbalance, I don't really experience

joy. There's no bright morning

in a bright summer. What strong
river or arm of wind. The moments,

when they do arrive on their slow boats,

fall apart as soon as the light
touches them. Always it's in

a car, always the windows down,

always the music too loud, it's never
apparent that none of us can sing.

The way cotton candy falls to its knees

at the suggestion of rain is the only thing
I've found to describe remembering,

after you've just been happy,

all the things that make you less
alive. This is the stone at the bottom

of the hill. This is the sapling and then,
later, the chainsaw. I have no reason
to be here again, windows down, ears

beginning to ring. There's nowhere

to go, and I'll be damned
if I ever get there.

PSALM 12, IN WHICH THE AUTHOR ALIENATES HIS AUDIENCE

I can no longer hide the way
I feel. Cats suck. Cats are

proof that Satan exists and wants us
to suffer. Cats are like if a cuddlier

animal, say a rabbit or a shark,
were very intent on breaking

all of your shit. Cats poop
in a box, walk on the poop, and then

walk on your kitchen counter.
Case closed.

PSALM 12, IN WHICH THE AUTHOR ALIENATES HIS AUDIENCE, PART 2

Wait I'm not done. Dogs have been known to call 911
for their owners. Your cat, your cat that

you love, would watch you bleed out
because it's curious what your face

tastes like. Your cat is the best thing
that happens in your day; your cat

is the best thing that happens in your cat's
day. If cats had a theme song it would be

"Break Stuff" by Limp Bizkit. Your cat,
I assume its name is some shit like

Wuffles or Pookie, resents what you
named it. Your cat calls itself Balthazarius,

Eater of Hearts and Fucker of Mothers.
Well, your cat calls itself "meow,"

but that's not here and neither is it
there. Listen, the point is, fuck
your cat, and fuck you.

LOSE THE FINGER

And now it's time to say goodbye
For the old pierhead's a-drawing nigh
–AMERICAN TRADITIONAL

So here's a sea shanty for the middle
⠀⠀⠀⠀⠀⠀of America. There's no rope
to haul on that will make the corn
⠀⠀⠀⠀⠀⠀slink by faster. The bottle

of rum is Coors or Fireball
⠀⠀⠀⠀⠀⠀but we drink it rough
all the same. My vessel is whatever
⠀⠀⠀⠀⠀⠀Ford or Honda they've seen fit

to deliver unto my hands and I pilot
⠀⠀⠀⠀⠀⠀it from port to port on no sleep
and caffeine and back pain, the calls
⠀⠀⠀⠀⠀⠀home are pigeons sent off

the bow with small assurance
⠀⠀⠀⠀⠀⠀of their return. Why would she answer
at one in the morning? I just need
⠀⠀⠀⠀⠀⠀to say goodnight. How far away

is Denver, my brother, I've not seen
⠀⠀⠀⠀⠀⠀a porch light for miles. Send beds.
If no beds, sleep on the floor. The trucks
⠀⠀⠀⠀⠀⠀on 35 sound suspiciously like waves.

ME, BUT HAPPY

I would like to thank you, personally,
for always making me feel like I'm cooler
than a wolf wearing sunglasses. When

I'm around you it's like I'm full of electricity
but in a fun, non-lethal way that's possibly
giving me a boner. I want to thank you

for making all the love songs
mean something again. Now when
Sam Smith comes on the radio

I still roll my eyes but I do it
while air humping. The best part
of being in love with you is

that I never HAVE to brush
my teeth, but gosh darn it do I
want to. You're the best thing

that's happened to me since I was,
like, born. You make me want to do
pointless, actually dumb things, like

learning to play the flute or voting.
In the list of things I love about you,
maybe the second or third entry

is the way you turn all my awful days
into awful days with cheeseburgers.
Have you ever smashed your face

into a whole bunch of cool, wet
sand? You should, cause that's pretty much
what it's like to hang out with you.

I've never made out with Jesus,
but I imagine that's kind of like
holding your hand. If I had scurvy,

it'd be all right because I'd have
scurvy with you. I'd clear the snow
off of twelve driveways in negative

twenty degree weather just so I could
leave you a voicemail. I would like to
thank you for never, not once,

making fun of me for crying while
I watch the same scene from *Parks and Rec*
for the twenty-fifth time. If you had it your way,

every day I would meet a puppy. Every
night would be trivia night. Every morning
I would get to wake up and punch

Ben Affleck in his stupid face.
I always try to be, like, cool
and stuff, but it's hard to act like I don't

care when you're so pretty
all the goddamn time. The new way
to say "I love you" is to just ram

our foreheads together. We can't really
be sad if we're both sad in the same place
right? I would like to thank you for wanting me

to be me, but happy. I don't know why
we're both here, but since we are, let's
make out until we're dead. Before I met you

I wanted to be dead all the time. I still do, because
of the, you know, mental illness, but now
that you're here I don't want to want to

die anymore. If you were a breakfast
cereal you'd be called "Reason-to-Wake-Up
Os." If you were a book you'd be titled

"Your Perfect Life, Right Here."
Sure, there are probably
infinite dimensions, but I'm

with you in this one, so why
would I try to find them?

WELCOME TO WALL DRUG

After I've already been through three
hundred miles of South Dakota, there
it is, waiting for me in the back of the town. Wall
Drug is a city block long and contains untold
wonders. Before you start, let me say that no one
is paying me for this, although please someone
pay me for this, I just
love it here. Wall Drug is what you hope
every other tourist trap is going to be.
There's an Old West Mall with creepy
statues whose express purpose is to pose
with you in pictures and also probably
play poker with each other at night. You can
pan for gold while you're "serenaded"
by a cross-eyed animatronic cowboy
band. Yes, the coffee is five cents
and yes the ice water is free. I'm mostly
excited to be here because, and not to diagnose
someone I've never met or really anyone
because I have no training and generally don't
know shit, but whoever designed this place was
clearly very mentally ill, or at least
in my head, so in my head it's great to see
that a crazy person can put together something
so successful and beloved. Often I wonder
if the things I think are important are just
shadows on a cave wall, the cave is blocked
by a boulder, the floor will soon all be
on fire. What if I build a house and all
the halls lead nowhere, a hundred rooms,
no beds, no windows, carpet on every
wall, what if what saves my life is only important
to me? Where do I go
when all the roads lead off the same

cliff? So where the heck is Wall Drug?
In some way, am I not always out there
in South Dakota, in the Badlands, picking
out bumper stickers, panning for gold,
needing to resume the drive home, but
where are the keys, where did I leave the car?

WISCONSIN TOWN

I hear that in Wisconsin everyone has wings
in their mouths. Dawn comes around 9:30. Whenever

it wakes up, really. In Wisconsin it never
rains. All the streets are paved with gold or something

like it. Maybe in Wisconsin they know
how to make bricks look like gold. Or maybe in Wisconsin

they have a lot of gold and aren't telling
anyone. In Wisconsin I love you. I've never been anywhere

but Wisconsin. Wisconsin is my ride
home. I hear that if you move to Wisconsin, all your sins

fall off. If you move to Wisconsin
all the friends you alienated suddenly remember

what they liked about you
and they help you move to Wisconsin. In Wisconsin

all the corn is so soft. Every bed
a field. In Wisconsin I never stopped.

GOING TO TEXAS

Not that there's anywhere to go
home to, but going home now is the same
as doing karaoke. All my friends
who I only see on occasions like this
(weddings, Thanksgiving, not Christmas,
funerals, mostly funerals) expect me to be
outlandish things like talented and cool.
They want James Brown splits and what
they're gonna get is Chris Farley. I drink
now, I didn't then, so that will help me
still not speak up when someone tries
to tell me I wasn't at the Glassjaw show
in '04 because who cares if I was, I thought
we measured success now by, you know,
success. There's a bottle of brandy
in my mother's pantry that for
five years has meant nothing
to anyone. There was a bottle but I found
it and now it's gone. Well it's not gone
it's just in pieces down the street. If there
were a home to go to I'd want to tell it
this: you should have taken me when
you had the chance. Now if I get someone
pregnant or kill myself it will have
been on purpose. I no longer take apart
what I cannot put back together. I don't
give myself black eyes when someone
else can do it for me.

GOING TO WALES

Since I've never been, I have
the privilege of imagining. You know
how every place is perfect until
you learn they're all places, and places
often contain people, and people,
as you know, are awful. So anyway,
I'm going to Wales and I'm pretty sure
that they are all dragons because I glean
all of my world knowledge from flags
and conjecture. Guessing is more fun
than knowing, which is the principal
problem with the internet. So anyway,
I was talking about Wales. In Wales
the roads all connect to each other,
all five of them. The eggs are all brown,
but a real warm brown, you know? You
could get married in any one of these
houses. Sure, I'll go there and it will
become real, someone will spit at me
and I'll see a mountain and I'll have
an incredible meal, the place will become,
you know, a place, but anyway
right now I'm inventing castles
and in one of them is a dragon.

THE FUTURE

The worst thing about being naked—and then
being hit by a car—is that road rash
is a problem for skin. Why was I naked
in the middle of the road at noon? I am glad
you asked, imaginary other half of this
conversation. I have no idea. Some characteristics

of bipolar disorder can include dissociation, hallucinations,
and fugue states, so sometimes I wake up in places
I didn't go to sleep. So, there I am, nude,
splayed out on the hood of a car like a slutty
chicken, and I'm screaming about the government
conspiracy to take away my feet. Not my real feet.

Just my brain feet. I'm about six inches away
from the concrete when I realize, in slow motion,
like the exact opposite of a rhinoceros attack,
"This is not how I imagined my life would turn out."

When I was little, I broke both
my ankles jumping off a roof because
I was sure a cape would enable me to fly. My parents
attributed this to my strong imagination. Last year,
my therapist called it a delusion. I fail

to see the difference. Also, I really can fly
and see the future and make stupid people leave
coffee shops with my mind. Forty-three percent of the time.
Sometimes I see people as colors. The point is,

here is a list of things my brain has told me
to do: join a cult; start a cult; become a cabinet maker;
kill myself, so, in essence, become a cabinet maker;

break into, and then paint, other people's houses; have sex
with literally everyone who reminds me of my mother;
fight animals that are much fightier than me, like
bears, so, in essence, kill myself. I think a lot

about killing myself, not like a point on a map but rather
like a glowing exit sign at a show that's never been
quite bad enough to make me want to leave. See, when I'm up
I don't kill myself because, holy shit, there's so much left

to do. When I'm down I don't kill myself because then
the sadness would be over, and the sadness is my old paint
under the new. The sadness is the house fire or the broken
shoulder: I'd still be me without it but I'd be so boring.

They keep telling me seeing things that aren't technically there
is called "disturbed cognitive functioning." I call it
"having a superpower." Once, I pulled over on the freeway
and jumped out of my old Jeep because I saw it burst
into flames twenty seconds before it actually burst
into flames. I knew my girlfriend and I would be

together because she turned bright pink the first time
she saw me. I know tomorrow is going to come
because I've seen it. Sunrise is going to come,
all you have to do is wake up. The future has been

at war, but it's coming home so soon; the future
is the map and the treasure; the future looks like
a child in a cape; the future is just like gravity:

everyone is slowly drifting toward everyone else,
we are all going to be part of each other
one day; the future is a blue sky and a full
tank of gas. I saw the future, I did,
and in it I was alive.

There are too many people to thank, and this space is too small to contain all my gratitude, so I will just say this: this book is for you, Anny. I almost lost you, but you let me find you again.

ABOUT THE AUTHOR

Neil Hilborn is a College National Poetry Slam champion and a 2011 graduate with honors from Macalester College. In 2013, his poems "OCD" and "The Future" went viral, garnering over 125 million combined views to date, making them among the most-viewed poems of all time. He has performed in 39 states and 7 countries, and in 2017 alone he traveled more than 50,000 miles to perform his poetry. Originally from Houston, Texas, he now lives in Saint Paul, Minnesota. *The Future* is Neil's second full-length poetry collection.

OTHER BOOKS BY BUTTON POETRY

If you enjoyed this book, please consider checking out some of our others, below. Readers like you allow us to keep broadcasting and publishing. Thank you!

Aziza Barnes, *me Aunt Jemima and the nailgun.*

J. Scott Brownlee, *Highway or Belief*

Nate Marshall, *Blood Percussion*

Sam Sax, *A Guide to Undressing Your Monsters*

Mahogany L. Browne, *smudge*

Neil Hilborn, *Our Numbered Days*

Sierra DeMulder, *We Slept Here*

Danez Smith, *black movie*

Cameron Awkward-Rich, *Transit*

Jacqui Germain, *When the Ghosts Come Ashore*

Hanif Willis-Abdurraqib, *The Crown Ain't Worth Much*

Aaron Coleman, *St. Trigger*

Available at *buttonpoetry.com/shop* and more!